TRANSATLANTICA

Kenny Finkle

I0139900

BROADWAY PLAY PUBLISHING INC
New York
www.broadwayplaypub.com
info@broadwayplaypub.com

Cover photo by Peter Hoerburger

First edition: December 2017
I S B N: 978-0-88145-745-2

Book design: Marie Donovan
Page make-up: Adobe InDesign
Typeface: Palatino

TRANSATLANTICA was first produced by The Flea Theater (Artistic Director, Jim Simpson; Producing Director, Carol Ostrow; Associate Producer, Erik Sniedze) opening on 23 April 2002. The cast and creative contributors were:

REGINALD.. Jack O'Neill
NATASHA .... Beth Tapper
ILYRIA .... Jennifer McKenna
UDI BOHE .... Alfredo Narciso
INSPECTOR STRANG-JAY .... Greg Keller
JACQUES JACQUES .... Dean Strange

Director .... Tim Cummings
Assistant director .... Mike Batistick
Set design & props .... Chris Skeens
Costumes .... Katherine Huang
Lights .... Shawn Gallagher
Sound .... Brian P J Cronin
Choreography .... Holly Handman
Fight choreography .... Jose Figueroa
Violinist .... Karen Lee Larson
Original music ....Tim Cummings & Karen Lee Larson
Deer maker .... Stacy Dawson
Stage manager .... Rebecca Gura

TRANSATLANTICA was subsequently presented by
The Operating Theater Company (Dori Ann Scagnelli
and Jason Schuler, Producers) in association with New
York Theatre Workshop, opening on 1 October 2010.
The cast and creative contributors were:

REGINALD.. Tim Donovan Jr
NATASHA ....Anna Foss Wilson
ILYRIA ....Evelyn Sullivan
UDI BOHE ....Keith Chandler
INSPECTOR STRANG-JAY ....Pierre-Marc Diennet
JACQUES JACQUES .... Eben Moore
various animals ....Mattieu Lorraine Dignard

Director ....Jason Schuler
Stage manager .... Helene Montagna
Set designer .... Gian Marco Lo Forte
Costume designer ....Jennifer Paar
Lighting designer ....Peter Hoerburger
Original music ....Mina Caputo & Ryan Oldenburg
Additional original music .... Rebecca Kupersmith
Sound designer .... Kim L Carter
Specialty taxidermy .... Ken Nintzel
Carpenter ....Jose Prieto
Scenic artist ....Carolyn Bonanni
Lighting board operator ....Josh Sturman
Marketing consultant ....Caroline Burwell
Marketing associate .... Dianne Short
Stage manager ....Helene Montagna

CHARACTERS & SETTING

DR REGINALD REINHOLD, *the greatest Doctor of the Mind in all of Transatlantica.*

NATASHA, *his wife*

ILYRIA, *a poetess of some note from the land of Ilyria*

UDI BOHE, *famous Theatre Director from the Land of Miscellenia, a close family friend of* REGINALD *and* NATASHA

INSPECTOR STRANG-JAY, *Transatlantica's Master Inspector,* REGINALD's *best friend.*

JACQUES JACQUES DEBUSSY DEBERGERAC, *a lot of people's one and only true love and* STRANGAY's *one and only true enemy*

THE DEER, *a Deer…*

A drawing room in Transatlantica—a continent of Upper Middle Earth. It is the turn of the century. Which century however, is not clear.

A note on language: With the exception of UDI BOHE *and* ILYRIA *all characters speak in some version of a mid-atlantic/ transatlantic accent.* ILYRIA *speaks with a tinge of cockney.*

(A drawing room in Transatlantica a continent of Upper Middle Earth, It is the turn of the century. Which century however, is not clear. ILYRIA *[Illa-ria] sits facing* REGINALD REINHOLD.*)*

REGINALD: And how does that make you feel?

ILYRIA: Horrible. Naturally.

REGINALD: Naturally.

ILYRIA: Though I suppose Death is natural.

REGINALD: Yes it is.

ILYRIA: And human.

REGINALD: Yes. Very.

ILYRIA: Oh to not be human!

REGINALD: Unfortunately—

ILYRIA: It's not an option I know.

REGINALD: No it's not.

ILYRIA: One day perhaps.

REGINALD: Perhaps. But not today.

ILYRIA: And today is it, isn't it?

REGINALD: For you, yes it is… And how does that make you feel?

ILYRIA: Horrible. Naturally.

REGINALD: Naturally.

ILYRIA: There is no tomorrow and tomorrow for me.

REGINALD: Speaking of which if you don't mind I'd appreciate payment in cash this week.

ILYRIA: Why so?

REGINALD: Well there's no telling when I'll see you again.

ILYRIA: Yes I suppose that's true.

REGINALD: And if a check bounced...

ILYRIA: I see your point. Unfortunately I don't have a penny on me.

REGINALD: Oh dear.

ILYRIA: Where?

REGINALD: Pardon?

ILYRIA: Where is the Deer? I love Deer. So noble and majestic. If only all Life imitated a Deer.

REGINALD: No, no, I simply meant "oh dear" as in "oh no". There is no Deer here.

ILYRIA: Oh cruel cruel world!

(Silence. We hear the clock ticking. It's exaggerated.)

ILYRIA: I suppose it isn't so bad.

REGINALD: What?

ILYRIA: Dying.

REGINALD: Oh?

ILYRIA: Well, I'm just so bored.

REGINALD: With what?

ILYRIA: With Life naturally.

REGINALD: Naturally.

ILYRIA: Every moment leads to another and then another. And for what? In the end waits Death, so Life I declare is boring and I for one am happy to be going. Bon Voyage Life!

REGINALD: This seems to be a breakthrough of some sort.

ILYRIA: Yes I believe it is.

REGINALD: And how does that make you feel?

ILYRIA: Wonderful. Naturally.

REGINALD: Naturally.

ILYRIA: Of course now that I feel wonderful I don't want to die. How much Time do I have left?

REGINALD: Twelve minutes.

ILYRIA: Ah Time. Dwindling away as we speak.

REGINALD: Yes.

ILYRIA: Summers fly, winters walk.

REGINALD: Yes.

ILYRIA: All's well that ends well.

REGINALD: Yes.

ILYRIA: Today is the first day of the rest of my life.

REGINALD: Yes.

ILYRIA: Addendum. Today is the last day of the rest of my Life. Ah! Aren't I witty? Even facing the fangs of outrageous fortune, I still find Life's humor squeezed out like blood from a rock.

REGINALD: Powerful imagery.

ILYRIA: Well I am a poetess of some note.

REGINALD: Yes.

ILYRIA: B natural.

REGINALD: Pardon?

ILYRIA: That is the note I am a poetess of.

REGINALD: I don't follow.

ILYRIA: I don't either. I lead. I always lead.

REGINALD: Oh dear.

ILYRIA: Where is the Deer? I love Deer. So noble and majestic. If only all Life imitated the Deer.

(The door swings open. It's NATASHA.*)*

REGINALD: Natasha!

NATASHA: So sorry to intrude Reginald. Hello.

ILYRIA: Hello. I'm Ilyria of the land of Ilyria.

NATASHA: Natasha. Reginald's wife. *(Way dramatic)* Oh life!

REGINALD: Is everything alright Natasha?

NATASHA: No Reginald, nothing's alright.

REGINALD: What is it darling?

NATASHA: Well Reginald, I'm dying.

ILYRIA: Me too!

REGINALD: What?

ILYRIA and NATASHA: I'm dying.

REGINALD: *(To* ILYRIA*)* I know you are. But you Natasha?

NATASHA: Yes I'm dying.

REGINALD: And how does that make you feel?

NATASHA: Horrible. Naturally.

REGINALD: Naturally. And when did you find this out?

NATASHA: Years ago. As a little girl. My mother told me.

REGINALD: Told you what?

NATASHA: That Death would one day take me.

REGINALD: Darling that is a figurative phrase. Death takes us all one day.

NATASHA: Yes.

REGINALD: So you're not sick?

NATASHA: No. But I am dying.

REGINALD: But only in the abstract.

NATASHA: There is nothing abstract about Death Reginald.

REGINALD: Of course there is. Is Death at your door darling?

NATASHA: No.

REGINALD: Do you have the symptoms of Death?

NATASHA: No.

REGINALD: Then its pure abstraction. Remove it from your mind.

NATASHA: …It won't go away.

REGINALD: Damn. This seems to require a deeper probing, hmmm? How about we schedule an appointment for tomorrow say, around 3:19 in the pm?

NATASHA: That will be fine. But until then?

REGINALD: Remove it from your mind.

NATASHA: …I'll try darling.

REGINALD: That's all one can do, try. Life my dear is the process of trying.

NATASHA: And dying.

REGINALD: Well yes, I suppose but-

NATASHA: Oh Death! Oh Life! AHHHHHH!!!!!!!!!!!!!!!!!!!!

REGINALD: Natasha! You're flying into hysterics!

ILYRIA: What Time's her flight?

NATASHA: AHHHHHHHHHH!!!!!!!!!!!!!!!!!!!!!!!!!!!!!!!!!!!!!!

REGINALD: Natasha, this is going to hurt you more than it hurts me.

(REGINALD *slaps her across the face.*)

NATASHA: Oh my! Reginald, I fear I lost myself momentarily. Thank you for slapping me. I needed that slap. Oh darling! You're marvelous. I must kiss you!!!!! (*She starts to kiss* REGINALD.)

ILYRIA: Bravo! That was truly breathtaking! I've been told that Dr Reinhold is the best Doctor of the Mind in all of Transatlantica and now I see that it is true.

(*A buzzer goes off.*)

REGINALD: Your Time's up Ilyria.

ILYRIA: Have truer words ever been said? You see Natasha, I've only just arrived in Transatlantica and now due to circumstances beyond my control I will be leaving Transatlantica and disintegrating into the Earth.

NATASHA: Yes, well have a safe trip.

REGINALD: Yes Ilyria. Keep your chin up, hmmm?

ILYRIA: I will. Thank you. Even as I die. I will. Of course it would all be so much easier with my one and only true love, Jacques Jacques Debussy Debergerac by my side!!!!

NATASHA: Jacques Jacques Debussy Debergerac did you say?

ILYRIA: Yes! Jacques Jacques Debussy Debergerac, my one and only true love. I received word through the daisy chain that Jacques Jacques was returning home to Transatlantica and beating a path here to Casa May We Siboplay or Rue De La Macon. Tell me Dr Reinhold, why does this Chateau have two names?

REGINALD: Actually, it's quite fascinating. The King of Transatlantica at the time of the Chocki War, Henry Marcus Chevailler, used to use this Chateau for his lover trysts. In order to keep its true identity under wraps he named it Casa May We Siboplay. Inspired by his journeys the previous season to Francovania and Spaniblania, respectively.

ILYRIA: So it's true name is Rue de la Macon?

REGINALD: So you would think Ilyria, so you would think. But…The King not wanting his guise so easily stripped, threw in a wrench.

ILYRIA: Where'd he throw it? Is it still on the land? It must have historical consequences.

REGINALD: No, no no. Not a real wrench, a figurative wrench.

ILYRIA: A figurative wrench…is that anything like a hammer?

REGINALD: No

ILYRIA: I'm afraid you've lost me.

REGINALD: Precisely. That was King Henry's exact intention. You see Ilyria the path to the truth is never simple.

ILYRIA: That's so true, so very true, or is it? Perhaps when Jacques Jacques arrives, Jacques Jacques will know.

NATASHA: Oh this can't be! Jacques Jacques! Returning here! Oh Jacques Jacques! Here after all this Time. Oh Jacques Jacques, Jacques Jacques, Jacques Jacques, Jacques Jacques, Jacques Jacques, Jacques Jacques, Jacques Jacques, Jacques Jacques. Not a day goes by that I don't think on you.

REGINALD: So are you saying Natasha that you'd welcome Jacques Jacques back?

NATASHA: Well darling of course, you don't shut the door on your one and only true love. You open it wide and deep.

REGINALD: But what of us? Don't you love me?

NATASHA: Never! I find you repulsive!

REGINALD: Surely Jacques Jacques can't just waltz in-

NATASHA: Jacques Jacques does not waltz!

ILYRIA: Oh yes Jacques Jacques does. Jacques Jacques waltzes and tangoes and sambas and rumbas and even does a bit of modern ballet.

NATASHA: Jacques Jacques? Ha! You must be mistaken! My Jacques Jacques never dared step foot on a dance floor.

ILYRIA: Jacques Jacques doesn't step on anyone's feet now either. Jacques Jacques is as graceful as a wasp.

(Beat)

NATASHA: Darling, I'm famished. Might you whip up some sort of sociable with a lovely whipped cream on it, hmmm?

REGINALD: Very well. I will return ladies. Don't talk too much about me now!

NATASHA: Don't worry darling, we aren't going to talk about you at all.

REGINALD: I didn't think you would. (He exits.)

NATASHA: Tell me Ilyria, precisely how long do you have to live?

ILYRIA: Precisely is a very precise word Natasha and Life and Death and Time as you know are quite imprecise. Death may take me at any Time.

NATASHA: What about right now?

(NATASHA lunges for ILYRIA and starts strangling her. ILYRIA screams.)

NATASHA: Jacques Jacques Debussy Debergerac is my one and only true love and I won't share Jacques Jacques with another.

ILYRIA: I don't mind sharing!

NATASHA: I do.

ILYRIA: I don't.

(*Suddenly a shot rings out from offstage.*)

ILYRIA: What was that?

(REGINALD *rushes into the room with a platter of sociables with whipped cream on them.*)

REGINALD: Lawrence, the strapping butler has shot himself in the ear. He's dead.

NATASHA: Oh dear!

ILYRIA: Where?

NATASHA: Where's Lawrence's body?

REGINALD: On the lawn Natasha, right next to the freshly planted petifores. But I highly suggest you that you refrain—

NATASHA: I must see him.

ILYRIA: I must as well.

(NATASHA *and* ILYRIA *run to the window, and pull back the curtains. Suddenly a letter flies in through the window.*)

NATASHA: Why look! It's a letter! From Lawrence. Addressed to me! From the grave!

REGINALD: Give me that.

NATASHA: Never! And now I must read it.

(NATASHA *opens the letter and music starts. She suddenly has a very private musical moment.*)

NATASHA: (*Singing*) No!!!!!!!!!!!!!!!
How can this be?

Why must this news come to me?
But why do I care?…
I must love him more than I can bear.
I will feign confusion…now.

(Beat)

REGINALD: Well?

NATASHA: I can't make heads or tales of it. *(She puts the letter into her bodice.)* I still need to see Lawrence's body!

ILYRIA: I as well.

(ILYRIA and NATASHA look back out the window.)

ILYRIA & NATASHA: AHHHHHHH!!!! Oh Death!

NATASHA: You cruel cruel Master!

ILYRIA: So beautiful! And ugly!

NATASHA: Take me you fool!

ILYRIA: I feel you in my brain, swishing around!

NATASHA: Take me and be done with me! I am now forever dead.

ILYRIA & NATASHA: Farewell.

ILYRIA: —to this world and the next.

(Simultaneously, NATASHA clasps her heart and ILYRIA grabs her head and they start to stumble about the room and then fall to the ground.)

REGINALD: Hello? Hello there ladies? Natasha? Ilyria? Hello? Are you both dead? Hello? Oh damn. What to do. Hmmm? I know. Of course. *(He picks up the phone and dials.)* Hello Police Precinct it's Dr Reginald Reinhold at Rue de la Macon or the Casa May We Siboplay… Ah hello Bedelia. A problem with Thomas? What did you say? And what did he say? And then what did you say? And then what did he say? Aha. And how does that make you feel? Aha. Yes. Precisely. Well ring around in the morrow, I have a free slot

at 4:23 in the P M and we'll sort it all out then. Yes.
Alright. My pleasure Bedelia. Cheerio. *(He hangs up.
A beat. He's satisfied. Another problem solved. Then—)*
Oh damn. *(He dials again)* Ah hello Bedelia it's Dr
Reinhold again. At the Rue de la Macon or the Casa
May We Siboplay. I see. Well have you tried talking
about it? Enough Bedelia! This isn't about you! I am
calling under the most horrible of circumstances. Well
it is not for you to know. Inspector Strang-jay in?
Yes well will you please tell him to ring round when
he has a chance. Oh nothing really. Lawrence the
strapping butler shot himself in the ear. He's dead. Yes.
Unfortunate. Madame Reinhold may be dead as well.
Yes and Mademoiselle Ilyria. Of the land of Ilyria. She
just arrived today. Yes, she may be dead as well. It's
too soon to tell really. Very well. Alright. Cheerio.

(Both ILYRIA *and* NATASHA *come to and are sitting up.)*

REGINALD: Ah! You're both alive.

ILYRIA & NATASHA: We are?

REGINALD: Yes. Hello.

ILYRIA & NATASHA: We are.

REGINALD: Yes. And how does that make you feel?

ILYRIA & NATASHA: Wonderful. Naturally.

REGINALD: Naturally.

ILYRIA: Oh Life! To be alive. To live. To feel. To move.
Life is for the living!

(The sun goes down suddenly.)

NATASHA: Goodbye fair sun.

(The moon comes up....)

NATASHA: Hello kind moon. *(She begins to cry.)*

REGINALD: What is it Natasha?

NATASHA: It's just all so meaningless.

REGINALD: What is darling?

NATASHA: Life. Love. Despair. Emotion. Thought. Action. Death. Listen. All around us is the despair of Life. Listen! Now!

(Everyone's quiet. A crash of thunder)

ILYRIA: I hear thunder!

(It starts to rain.)

ILYRIA: I hear rain!

NATASHA: Rain! I love a fabulous rainstorm.

ILYRIA: That's not just rain Natasha. That is an omen! A bad one at that!

NATASHA: Well what could it mean?

ILYRIA: It means its an omen. A bad one at that!

REGINALD: I'm sure you're over-reacting Ilyria. Rain is just rain is just rain is just rain. *(He walks to the window.)* That's odd!

ILYRIA: What is it?

REGINALD: Lawrence's body has just disintegrated into the Earth in front of my very eyes.

NATASHA: Impossible!

REGINALD: I just saw it, with my very own eyes.

NATASHA: Let me see.

REGINALD: Darling there's nothing to see. He disintegrated.

(NATASHA rushes to the window. ILYRIA rushes up as well.)

NATASHA: Why, he's gone! What could it mean?

ILYRIA: It means it's an omen. A bad one at that.

(The doorbell chimes. It's ominous.)

ILYRIA: What's that?

REGINALD: The door.

ILYRIA: The door?

REGINALD: Yes someone's at the door.

ILYRIA: Maybe its Jacques Jacques!

NATASHA: Jacques Jacques. Jacques Jacques. Jacques Jacques. Jacques Jacques. Jacques Jacques. Jacques Jacques. Jacques Jacques. Jacques Jacques. Oh Deer!

ILYRIA: Where?

NATASHA: Right outside that window! A Deer is staring in at us!

ILYRIA: Let me see!

(Sure enough, there really is a DEER *looking in.)*

ILYRIA: Why look at that! Hello! Hello Deer I've been trying to see you all day! My you are lovely!

(The doorbell again. This Time its even more ominous.)

REGINALD: Er—I'll get it.

*(*REGINALD *opens the door. In walks a very wet* UDI BOHE, *Famous Theatre Director from the land of Miscellanea.)*

REGINALD: Why look it is Udi Bohe Famous Theatre Director from the land of Miscellanea!

UDI: *(He has a strange and unidentifiable accent:)* In ze Seatre zare ees no rain, only pain!

NATASHA: Oh Udi it's you!

UDI: Zee vun und only. Und who are you?

ILYRIA: I can't understand a word you're saying.

REGINALD: Yes well Udi Bohe this is Ilyria of the land of Ilyria. Ilyria, Udi, to be repetitive, is a famous director of Theatre from the land of Miscellanea.

UDI: Yah boot I vas exiled und now leave en Transatlantica ven I'm not vorking. Right now I em not vorking. Dis ees an issue of great sensitivity to may und I'd appreciet eet eef vu deedn't mension eet et ell.

ILYRIA: I'm not quite sure I got what you said. Regardless. I love the Theatre with all my heart. I go everytime I'm near one. Are you working on anything right now?

UDI: *(Crumbling to his knees)* Ooh! Vu crull crull criture! Vu vamp! Vu!

ILYRIA: Did I say something wrong?

UDI: Vu sed vat vu meant. Een zee Seatre zare are no wrongs, only absolutes!

ILYRIA: What?

UDI: Een zee Seatre

ILYRIA: Een, zee, Seatre. None of those are words I've ever heard. Where are you from?

UDI: Miscellanea.

ILYRIA: Where is that?

UDI: Af de coas of Chiemlasser Strasse Propahere.

(ILYRIA *suddenly clutches her head and starts to stumble around the room.*)

ILYRIA: I'm afraid all this deciphering is bringing me to Death's door! Hello! Death! I feel you in my brain, swishing around! Aha! It is here! Farewell to this world and hello the next. *(She falls to the ground and dies.)*

UDI: Is she dade?

NATASHA: One can only hope.

REGINALD: Only Time will tell.

UDI: A vez. Time. Oh Time. If only dare vas more of eet.

REGINALD: Yes. Please have a seat. I'll make you a drink.

UDI: Yes a dreenk! Meex eet wit hope!

NATASHA: What brings you out in the midst of a rainstorm Udi?

UDI: Veil I just cem from my Doctor cwho told me dat my medication eesn't vorking and I vas going to die very soon. Pairhaps today pairhaps in feefty years. Novun knows fer shore. So to ease my pain I vent to zee park acroos da vay to heve sex wit strangers. Dat alvays meks me feel more alive.

REGINALD: Now Udi, you know we've been through this before in your sessions. The sensation of anonymous sex makes you feel more anonymous, more invisible, in essence, closer to Death.

UDI: Vell, I knew I vas getting closer to somesing.

NATASHA: Udi, I suppose this is as a good a Time as any to tell you that I am dying as well.

UDI: No!

NATASHA: Yes!

REGINALD: Natasha, now we've already been through this. You are not dying.

NATASHA: Yes I am! I'm dying! Dying. Dying. Dying.

UDI: Oh! Da humanity of eet all! Let's hold each other!

NATASHA: Yes. Let's.

(They do. NATASHA begins to cry.)

NATASHA: Oh Udi! There's even more Death surrounding us.

UDI: Vat?

NATASHA: Lawrence is dead!

UDI: Ded?

NATASHA: Yes. He shot himself.

REGINALD: In the ear.

UDI: Thru zee ear! Mein got! Quel dramatique! Peety abut Lawrence, I chad heem often.

NATASHA: I as well. Oh Lawrence! We'll never know the complex workings of your complex heart! Thank the heavens Jacques Jacques Debussy Debergerac is returning. I just pray Jacques Jacques returns before I die.

(Thunder rolls.)

UDI: Jacques Jacques Debussy Debergerac ees returning? Oh Jacques Jacques! Jacques Jacques! Jacques Jacques! Jacques Jacques!

REGINALD: You mean to tell me that you would welcome Jacques Jacques back as well?

UDI: But of course. Jacques Jacques vas my vun und only true luf. Vu do not turn your back on luf! Vu velcome eet en vide und dep.

REGINALD: But surely Jacques Jacques can't just waltz in—

NATASHA & UDI: Jacques Jacques does not waltz!!

REGINALD: According to Ilyria, he waltzes and tangoes and sambas and rumbas and even does a bit of modern ballet.

UDI: My Jacques Jacques? Ha! You must be mistaken.

(NATASHA suddenly attacks UDI and starts strangling him.)

NATASHA: Jacques Jacques is my one and only true love and I won't share Jacques Jacques with another.

UDI: I don't mind sharing!

NATASHA: I do.

UDI: I don't.

(ILYRIA suddenly wakes up.)

ILYRIA: I don't mind sharing either.

REGINALD: Ilyria! Thank heavens, you're still alive.

ILYRIA: I am? I am! Oh Life! To live it! Now, in honor of Life's strange fruit and wicked game if you don't mind I'd like to play the harp.

REGINALD: You play?

ILYRIA: Play what?

REGINALD: The harp.

ILYRIA: The harp what?

REGINALD: You play the harp.

ILYRIA: I was planning to. No need for demands.

REGINALD: No one's played this for years.

ILYRIA: Will No One mind if I use it?

REGINALD: No, not No One as in—I don't think No one will mind at all.

ILYRIA: Good. *(She sits at the harp and begins to play. She's good. Then she begins to sing. A real songbird)*
ILYRIA: Let me tickle your fancy
Let me trip on your wood
Let me be a bit chancy
Let me do what I would
I'm a little bit sassy
I'm a little bit tart
I've been told I am classy
Though on occasion I fart
If your heart is all broken
If you're down on your luck
Let me tickle your fancy
I give a good (whoops!)
Let me tickle your fancy
Let me sit on your stick
I once was named Nancy
You once were named Mick

(They all applaud.)

REGINALD: Well Ilyria that was quite beautiful.

ILYRIA: Thank you, it's called "Hollow Heart".

REGINALD: Interesting. I would've thought its name would be "Let Me Tickle Your Fancy"

ILYRIA: Why?

REGINALD: Well you say that several times in the song.

ILYRIA: I don't think I say the word "that" at all in the song.

(Beat)

REGINALD: No I don't believe you do.

UDI: Das vas un slicay of cheaven. Tell me Mademoiselle vud vu be enterested een co-viting un scenario con mi? *(Beat)* Ah! I'll geeve vu un momenta un to tink about eet, yah? Ven vu chev un answer find may at zee bar…. *(He steps away, mixing himself another drink at the bar but watching the whole Time.)*

ILYRIA: What did he say?

REGINALD: He wondered if you would be interested in writing a scenario with him.

NATASHA: It's really quite an honor Ilyria. Udi is known throughout the world for his infamous scenarios. Did you ever hear of "The Fable of the Fallacious Feline"?

ILYRIA: No.

REGINALD: Or, "The Way to a Woman's Heart Is Not Through Her Trousers But Through Her Knickers"?

ILYRIA: No.

NATASHA: Say yes to him Ilyria. He's dying you know.

ILYRIA: He is?

NATASHA: Yes he just found out.

ILYRIA: I'm dying as well. Any minute I could go.

NATASHA: I know.

ILYRIA: Oh alright. *(She walks to* UDI.*)* Yes Mr Bohe. Yes. In honor of our imminent deaths I will proudly join your side in one last ache of creation before we make our lengthy and beautiful exit into the nether regions of existence.

UDI: Vat?

REGINALD: She said yes Udi, old boy. Yes.

UDI: Eggcellent! Oh gooty gooty!

(Thunder again)

UDI: Chall ye repair to zee udder room and get to work Ilyria?

ILYRIA: What?

REGINALD: He wants to know if you want to work in the other room.

ILYRIA: Very well the other room.

UDI: Ve vill only return ven our maestervork ees complete!

(The two leave. NATASHA *starts to leave as well,* REGINALD *blocks her way.)*

REGINALD: Where are you going my darling?

NATASHA: I must go upstairs to lie down and wait.

REGINALD: Wait for what?

NATASHA: Either Jacques Jacques or Death.

REGINALD: Natasha, what do you need of either of those tonight, hmmm?

NATASHA: They are all I have to live for Reginald.

REGINALD: But what of us? Don't you love me?

NATASHA: HA!!! Never! I find you repulsive!

REGINALD: But darling, I thought you truly loved me. What about Antwerp?

NATASHA: That wasn't me. I sent along a body double.

REGINALD: A body double?

NATASHA: Yes. It cost me an arm and a leg but I got new ones off the black market for half price.

REGINALD: I'm stunned Natasha. All this Time I've been living a lie.

NATASHA: Well Reginald, the path to a lie is always simple.

REGINALD: Yes I suppose it is. I feel like such a fool. And how does that make you feel?

NATASHA: I think the more important question is, how does that make *you* feel?

REGINALD: Fascinating! Evading my question with another question. What do you have to say to that?

NATASHA: That perhaps you were the one evading the question. Like always Reginald. Life is for living, not processing! And you may very well want to start living your Life Reginald. For who's to say where Death is at any given moment? Look at Lawrence case in point, hmmm? If I were you I'd cherish every moment as if it were your last, for it may be Reginald. It just may be.

REGINALD: What are you saying Natasha?

NATASHA: Just what I said. And now I must bid you adieu. *(She exits grandly.)*

REGINALD: Adieu.

(The DEER *reappears in the window.)*

REGINALD: Oh, Deer! What are you doing here? Staring in so? Hmmm? Do you have a secret perhaps? A secret in your silence. Hmm, the silence of the Deer. No, that doesn't sound quite right.....

(A beat. Then—the door again. REGINALD *opens it. It's* INSPECTOR STRANG-JAY.)

STRANG-JAY: Ah, Reginald! Good evening. So sorry I'm late but Time waits for no one.

REGINALD: It's alright Strang-jay old man, come in, please. Care for a drink?

STRANG-JAY: Yes. A Gimlet Transatlantica heavy on the irony.

REGINALD: Coming right up.

STRANG-JAY: So Lawrence shot himself hmmm?

Thunder!

REGINALD: Yes. In the ear.

STRANG-JAY: Probably was aiming for his heart.

REGINALD: His heart?

STRANG-JAY: Yes, happens all the Time, mistaking your head for your heart.

*(*REGINALD *hands* STRANG-JAY *the drink.)*

STRANG-JAY: Ah, thank you Reginald. Pity, about Lawrence, I had him often. As an emergency substitute for a female naturally. But my what forceps!

REGINALD: Forceps?

STRANG-JAY: Yes, he had twice as many muscles in his arms than any other human on Earth. It was documented by Doctor Favreau one balmy afternoon. Fascinating hmmm?

REGINALD: I had no idea.

STRANG-JAY: From the gardening I suppose…. Any signs of foul play?

REGINALD: No.

STRANG-JAY: Damn. I love a good intrigue. Enough evidence to frame an innocent perhaps?

REGINALD: No.

STRANG-JAY: Oh well, Life and its dreary details. Where's the body then?

REGINALD: The body?

STRANG-JAY: Yes, Lawrence's strapping frame. Where is it?

REGINALD: Hmmm?

STRANG-JAY: Lawrence's body. Where is it?

REGINALD: What's that?

STRANG-JAY: You're hiding something! What is it?

(Beat)

REGINALD: Damn you're good man!

STRANG-JAY: Aha!

REGINALD: Well Strang-jay it's the strangest thing. His body was lying out in the garden right next to the freshly planted petifores and then it disintegrated.

STRANG-JAY: Oh dear.

REGINALD: Yes, it keeps showing up.

STRANG-JAY: Whom?

REGINALD: The Deer.

STRANG-JAY: There is no Deer here. Is there?

REGINALD: Yes, right at the bay window.

STRANG-JAY: Why yes there is. And to think I was only exclaiming! Ah Life, so full of possibility! Now, I will recite the next portion of information in rhyme. A disintegrating body. A stormy night. Deer in the window. My what a fright. Now all we need. To complete this mystery. Is the shocking sound of a woman's scream.

REGINALD: The shocking sound of a woman's scream?

STRANG-JAY: Yes.

REGINALD: Why so?

STRANG-JAY: I don't know. I just know it's right.

REGINALD: Fascinating the way the mind of an Inspector works. Pure instinct.

STRANG-JAY: Yes Reginald, pure instinct, the gift of Life. To Instinct!

REGINALD: To Instinct!

(REGINALD *and* STRANG-JAY *clink glasses.*)

(*Suddenly lightning strikes and the* DEER *is illuminated in the window.*)

STRANG-JAY: Ah!

REGINALD: It was only the Deer.

STRANG-JAY: Draw the curtains! Quickly! That Deer terrifies me supremely.

REGINALD: And why do you think it does Strang-jay?

STRANG-JAY: Why what?

(REGINALD *suddenly has his pad and pen, taking notes.*)

REGINALD: Why does the Deer terrify you?

STRANG-JAY: I'm not quite sure.

REGINALD: And how does that make you feel?

STRANG-JAY: Terrible. Naturally.

REGINALD: Naturally. *(Beat)* Tell me, are you dying?

STRANG-JAY: Good god no I am the very picture of health. My Doctor just told me so previously. I am the very picture of health he said and should live to the ripe old age of a hundred and twenty-nine give or take fifty years. (*Suddenly he gets up, grabbing his stomach. He stumbles forward and then falls over—dead.*)

REGINALD: Strang-jay? Hello? Oh my. Oh damn.

(STRANG-JAY *then starts to laugh hysterically.*)

STRANG-JAY: Just a little joke Reggie! Ha ha ha! You see I had just said I am the very picture of health and should live to the ripe old age of a hundred and twenty-nine give or take fifty years and then I proceeded to die.

REGINALD: I say, you did get my goat there old man!

STRANG-JAY: Well what is Life if not for a joke or two, hmmm?

REGINALD: I couldn't agree more. And yet…

STRANG-JAY: Yes?

REGINALD: Fascinating that the Time that you've decided to joke was at an impasse regarding Life and Death.

STRANG-JAY: Yes. Fascinating. Naturally.

REGINALD: Naturally. (*He starts making some notes, as he does—*) Hmmm. Ha. Very interesting…

STRANG-JAY: What are you driving at?

REGINALD: Driving at?

STRANG-JAY: Yes, in your notes. And your silence. What is it?

REGINALD: Hmmm?

STRANG-JAY: You're driving at something. What is it?

(*Beat*)

REGINALD: Damn you're good man!

STRANG-JAY: Aha!

REGINALD: Well Strang-jay, it's the strangest thing. You see according to my notes and observations you disguise your fear of Death in a cloak of humor, denying your mortality and in essence heightening its awareness.

STRANG-JAY: Oh dear.

REGINALD: Yes it keeps showing up.

(A woman's shocking scream from offstage.)

ILYRIA: Ah! Thank heavens, the shocking sound of a woman's scream.

REGINALD: It sounded to me as if it were coming from the Master bedroom.

(A furious UDI *and* ILYRIA *rush in.)*

UDI: Vat vas dat?

STRANG-JAY: Ah hello there Udi Bohe. That my dear fellow was the shocking sound of a woman's scream.

ILYRIA: What is happening? I fear I don't understand.

STRANG-JAY: Allow me to explain.

ILYRIA: Who is Me?

STRANG-JAY: I'm me.

ILYRIA: Hello Me, I'm Ilyria.

STRANG-JAY: And I'm Inspector Strang-jay.

ILYRIA: I thought you said your name was Me?

STRANG-JAY: No I mean I was the me in question.

ILYRIA: I don't know where the land of Question is, is it near Ilyria?

STRANG-JAY: I don't know where Ilyria is.

ILYRIA: Why, I'm right here! Hello!

STRANG-JAY: Hello.

ILYRIA: Ilyria.

STRANG-JAY: Inspector Strang-jay.

ILYRIA: Pleasure to meet you. Oh I do like your use of words. Too bad you're not as stunning as Jacques Jacques.

STRANG-JAY: Jacques Jacques? Jacques Jacques. Jacques Jacques. Jacques Jacques. Jacques Jacques. Jacques Jacques. What makes you say that name?

ILYRIA: Jacques Jacques is my one and only true love.

UDI: Mine as vell.

STRANG-JAY: Jacques Jacques, that stunning scoundrel! After all this Time! Ha!

REGINALD: You don't mean to say that you Strang-jay would accept Jacques Jacques back as well?

STRANG-JAY: No ofcourse not. Jacques Jacques is my one and only true enemy. Tell me this Ilyria, how does that thorn in my side look?

ILYRIA: Jacques Jacques' face beats with the purest vitality of Life.

STRANG-JAY: Damn! The hands of Time have been cruel on the clay of my face and left Jacques Jacques' untarnished. You know while in academia we used to throw the shot putt together competitively. Jacques Jacques was always just a tad better, a smidge stronger, an inch or three longer!

(*A woman's shocking scream. Again*)

ILYRIA: Ah yes, the shocking sound of a woman screaming, I'd almost forgotten.

REGINALD: It sounded to me as if it were coming from the Master Bedroom.

STRANG-JAY: Aha! Now I will recite the next bit of information backwards. Explanation an is need we all now. Forgotten almost was that. Bedroom master the from scream a.

(*Beat. Everyone tries to decipher* STRANG-JAY'S *information.*)

REGINALD: An explanation?

STRANG-JAY: Yes.

REGINALD: Why so?

STRANG-JAY: I don't know. It just feels right.

(NATASHA *rushes in.*)

NATASHA: I fear my behavior requires explanation.

STRANG-JAY: Aha!

NATASHA: It was I who screamed twice with such fervor and terror. Two screams in the face of Death, which woke me from my slumber and beckoned me towards its greedy embrace! No I said! No! I am not ready! Death Death go away, come back some other day! If you don't I don't care! I will pull down your underwear!

STRANG-JAY: Good god woman, you said all that in the face of Death?

NATASHA: Yes!

STRANG-JAY: And where is Death now?

NATASHA: I lost him in the stairwell.

EVERYONE: Bravo! Job well done! So brave!

STRANG-JAY: You truly are a testament to the power of Life.

NATASHA: Yes. Life! I have won the battle. I have won for us all. We will live forever and a day! Eternity is ours! For Death will never ring our bell again.

(*The doorbell rings.*)

EVERYONE: (*But* REGINALD)
AHHHHHH!!!!!!!!!!!!!!!!!!!!!!!!!!!!

(REGINALD *goes to answer it, while the others hide behind the couch.*)

NATASHA: Where are you going Reginald? Hide behind the couch where it is safe.

REGINALD: I'm going to answer the door. What are you all afraid of?

EVERYONE: WHY, CAN'T YOU SEE IT MAN? IT'S DEATH COME A CALLING!

REGINALD: Don't be ridiculous. I'm sure it's a neighbor or a friendly traveler who has lost his way.

(REGINALD *opens the door. Standing there is DEATH. Or rather, the Mask of Death and a black cape.)*

REGINALD: AHHHHHH!!!

DEATH: AHHHHHH!!!

Everyone peaks their heads from behind the couch.

EVERYONE: AHHHHHHHHH!!

DEATH: AHHHHHHHHH!!!!!!!!!!!!!!!!!!!!!!!!!!!!!!!!!!!!!!

ILYRIA: Wait a minute. That scream sounds strikingly familiar.

NATASHA: Yes it reminds me of—

UDI: My vun und only—

STRANG-JAY: True enemy!

ALL: JACQUES JACQUES!

(DEATH *takes off it's mask. It's* JACQUES JACQUES *who's perfect, whatever that means.)*

REGINALD: Jacques Jacques. You've returned.

JACQUES JACQUES: Yes I have, haven't I? Sorry if the get up gave you a gasp... I just got back from the most fabulous costume ball in the outer Adirondockets. I went as Death. Apropos of course considering I'm dying.

ILYRIA: Not you as well Jacques Jacques?

JACQUES JACQUES: Yes I am afraid so. I have only the briefest Time left.

NATASHA: But how can Life be so unfair?

JACQUES JACQUES: Life simply can, because it can. I am terribly distraught over the whole thing. Dying seems like such an unappealing way to live, don't you agree?

ILYRIA: I couldn't agree more.

UDI: Chello dare Jacques Jacques my vun und only true luf. Eet ees me Udi Bohe. Vu probably don't recognize me. Vu see Death ches taken eets toll on me as veil. I em dying too.

ILYRIA: Me too.

NATASHA: Me too. Jacques Jacques Debussy Debergerac you are my one and only true love and I won't share you with another. In Life or Death.

(NATASHA *rushes for* JACQUES JACQUES. ILYRIA *and* UDI *rush as well. They end up in a heap on the floor in front of* JACQUES JACQUES.)

ILYRIA: I don't mind sharing.

UDI: Meen zeether!

NATASHA: I do.

ILYRIA & UDI: We don't.

NATASHA: Well you can't have Jacques Jacques. Jacques Jacques is mine. All mine! Tell them Jacques Jacques. Tell them. Tell them you refuse to share! Tell them my love, tell them!

JACQUES JACQUES: I refuse to share.

NATASHA: I knew it!

UDI: Boot Jacques Jacques vat aboot dat time een Giberia vit de Boy's Choir?

ILYRIA: And the Time with my three sisters and my seagull in the cherry orchard?

JACQUES JACQUES: Yes well all that is in the past. Death has made things clear for me. You see, I've only returned to Transatlantica with one goal in mind. And that goal is to finally win the heart of my one and only true love.

NATASHA: You already have my heart Jacques Jacques.

ILYRIA: Mine as well.

UDI: Mine too.

STRANG-JAY: Not mine you rogue!

JACQUES JACQUES: Ah Strang-jay, I barely recognized you. The hands of Time have truly been cruel to the clay of your face while leaving mine untarnished.

STRANG-JAY: You Jacques Jacques are my one and only true enemy and now I must kill you. (*He takes out a revolver.*)

ALL: AHHHHHHH!!!!!!!!!!!!!!!!!!!!!!!

JACQUES JACQUES: A revolver!

STRANG-JAY: Yes. Precisely. Fare. Thee. Well Jacques Jacques!

(STRANG-JAY *shoots* JACQUES JACQUES.)

JACQUES JACQUES: You shot me! In the heart!

REGINALD: Well done Strang-jay.

STRANG-JAY: Thank you Reggie old boy, unfortunately I was aiming for his ear. Common mistake.

JACQUES JACQUES: I'm dying! Dying! And now I will Dance a Complex Dance of Death!!!!!!! (*He begins waltzing.*)

ALL: Jacques Jacques is waltzing! (*Now a tango*).And tangoing. (*Now a samba*) And sambaing. (*Now a rumba*) And rumbaing as well (*And now a little bit of modern ballet*) And now even a bit of modern ballet!

ILYRIA: I told you so!!!!!

(JACQUES JACQUES *finishes. Bows. They all applaud.*
JACQUES JACQUES *falls to the floor.*)

NATASHA: Is Jacques Jacques?

UDI: Jacques Jacques can't be!

ILYRIA: Jacques Jacques mustn't! Jacques Jacques are
you dead?

JACQUES JACQUES: *(Popping up)* Not yet! But soon! Oh
the pain! Oh Death! If only I could die in the arms of
my one and only true love.

NATASHA: I'm here darling! Here I am!

ILYRIA: I'm right here!

UDI: Me too!

JACQUES JACQUES: No no no! None of you are my one
and only true loves!

UDI, NATASHA & ILYRIA: We're not?

JACQUES JACQUES: No!

ALL: Then who is?

JACQUES JACQUES: Lawrence.

ALL: Oh dear.

(DEER *appears in the window.*)

ILYRIA: Hello Deer!

JACQUES JACQUES: What is it?

NATASHA: Well Jacques Jacques, my one and only true
love, you see—

UDI: Lawrence ches shot heemself een ze ear.

STRANG-JAY: Though I believe that he was aiming for
his heart.

REGINALD: And then disintegrated into the Earth.

(JACQUES JACQUES *begins to cry.*)

JACQUES JACQUES: NO!!!!!! *(A la Stanley Kowalski)*
LAWRENCE!!!!!!!!!!!!!!! Oh Life! Why must it sting so
bad? *(He begins to die.)*

NATASHA, ILYRIA & UDI:	STRANG-JAY:
Jacques Jacques, don't die!!!!	Die Jacques Jacques, die!!!

JACQUES JACQUES: No! I must…

NATASHA: Then I fear I must too.

REGINALD: Natasha, you're not dying! None of you are!

JACQUES JACQUES: I am!

REGINALD: Well yes I suppose you are.

ILYRIA: I as well.

UDI: Same chere. Ilyria! Remember dee pain! Ve vill
use it een our scenario.

NATASHA: Death comes in all shapes and sizes
Reginald. And we are all truly dying. Now let us die in
peace. Or turmoil. Or both.

*(They take an exceedingly long time to die. Everything is
ultra dramatic. When they are all finally dead—)*

STRANG-JAY: I say Reginald this is quite satisfactory.
Jacques Jacques dying and all. Pity about the others
though.

REGINALD: Are they all truly dead?

STRANG-JAY: Well Reginald, the path to the truth is
never simple…. Very well, I'm off.

REGINALD: Off?

STRANG-JAY: Yes going on holiday to the south of
Asbestas with my Mistress. Her name is Citronella.

REGINALD: I had no idea.

STRANG-JAY: Yes. I've loved her from afar for far too long. But you see, she is dying and only has a questionable amount of Time left to live so we both felt that we should seize the day. After all, there may not be another. Fare. Thee. Well. Reginald I'm going to leave my hat behind however so that I will be forced to return momentarily to retrieve it.

REGINALD: Why so Strang-Jay?

STRANG-JAY: I don't know. I simply know it's right.

REGINALD: Yes of course Strang-Jay, good day.

(STRANG-JAY *opens the door… There is a snow storm raging outside.*)

STRANG-JAY: (*Screaming over the sound of the storm*) Good god! It's an inappropriate typhoon like blizzard of epic proportions! Good day!!!!!!!!!!!!!!!!

(STRANG-JAY *is gone.* REGINALD *looks at the bodies around him.*)

REGINALD: And Life beats on I suppose. Ho hum.

(*Suddenly* NATASHA *simply sits up.*)

REGINALD: Natasha!

NATASHA: Reginald. So good to see you. Hello.

REGINALD: You're alive!

NATASHA: No Reginald. I've been reborn.

REGINALD: Reborn?

NATASHA: Yes I've been reborn in my previous form but with a whole new set of morals and ambitions as well as a better complexion.

REGINALD: And how does that make you feel?

NATASHA: Alive. Naturally.

REGINALD: Naturally.

(JACQUES JACQUES *sits up….*)

JACQUES JACQUES: I've been reborn.

NATASHA: Oh damn. Jacques Jacques.

JACQUES JACQUES: Natasha darling!

NATASHA: Jacques Jacques, leave me alone. I want nothing more to do with you.

REGINALD: Do you mean to say as one of your new ambitions and morals you have decided that Jacques Jacques is no longer your one and only true love?

NATASHA: Precisely.

REGINALD: So darling, then who is your one and only true love? Is it me?

NATASHA: I don't have a one and only true love in this Life.

JACQUES JACQUES: But, I changed my morals and ambitions so that you were my one and only true love.

NATASHA: Unfortunately you are a lifetime too late. I find you both repulsive.

REGINALD: Natasha, if you only allow me to speak with you and state my case of love.

NATASHA: Never!

REGINALD: Try to love me.

JACQUES JACQUES: Or in any case let me try to love you.

(JACQUES JACQUES *and* REGINALD *rush for* NATASHA. *She pulls out a long and impressive sword.*)

REGINALD: Heavens to Mergatroid, that sword is enormous!

NATASHA: En garde!

REGINALD: En-garde?

JACQUES JACQUES: Engarde!

REGINALD: Er- Engarde! Yes!

(JACQUES JACQUES and REGINALD both take out swords. They all duel. It is a grand duel and goes on for some time in intense silence, then—)

REGINALD: And how is the dueling making you both feel?

JACQUES JACQUES & NATASHA: Wonderful. Naturally.

REGINALD: Naturally. Care to elaborate?

JACQUES JACQUES & NATASHA: No.

REGINALD: Very well.

(The doorbell rings.)

REGINALD: I'll get it!

(REGINALD abandons the sword fight and opens the door.)

(It's STRANG-JAY. The snowstorm has passed, it is now pitch black outside, perhaps it even looks like a Black Hole.)

STRANG-JAY: So sorry to barge back in Reginald but I seemed to have misplaced my hat. My god! They're alive!

REGINALD: Reborn.

STRANG-JAY: Reborn?

REGINALD: Care for a drink Strang-jay?

STRANG-JAY: Yes ofcourse. I'll have a Sturm and Drang. Heavy on the Drang.

(REGINALD goes to get his drink. STRANG-JAY observes the duel.)

STRANG-JAY: Strang…and fascinating. I knew there was a reason for me to return.

NATASHA: Silence! A duel of epic proportions is underway.

STRANG-JAY: Well excuse me for living!

JACQUES JACQUES: *(To* NATASHA*)* You've trained well.
Yes! I have! Unfortunately you haven't trained well
enough!

(JACQUES JACQUES *strikes* NATASHA *in the arm.)*

NATASHA: Wounded! And now...parry thrust parry!

JACQUES JACQUES: Natasha darling it does you no good
to announce your moves before you do them.

NATASHA: It does if you lie!

(NATASHA *strikes* JACQUES JACQUES. *In the heart)*

JACQUES JACQUES: Good shot Natasha. Right in my
heart.

NATASHA: Precisely where I was aiming.

JACQUES JACQUES: And now I must die again. I have
only loved you Natasha. Only you. You. Only. You.
Fare. Thee. Well. Again. Until I am reborn. Again.
Adieu.

(JACQUES JACQUES *is dead.* NATASHA *begins to cry.)*

REGINALD: Natasha darling, what is it?

NATASHA: I fear that my ambitions were terribly wrong
and misguided. To kill your one true love for sport.
Why have I done this? What corrodes my soul so
deeply that cruelty is its only respite?

REGINALD: But darling, Jacques Jacques wasn't your
one and only true love. You said so yourself.

NATASHA: I was lying Reginald! And now for the soul
of my one and only true love, Jacques Jacques Debussy
Debergerac, I must now sacrifice mine. Fare. Thee.
Well. Until I am reborn. Again. I am coming lover. I am
coming to you. Adieu. *(She stabs herself and dies. She sits
up suddenly.)* I've been reborn. Again.

STRANG-JAY: Oh what fun!!!! I haven't had such an entertaining evening since the last time you died. Which strang..ly was just this evening!

NATASHA: It is no longer evening. It is morning again.

STRANG-JAY: Nonsense. It is pitch black outside.

NATASHA: Look again Strang-Jay.

(The sun has risen. It's morning.)

STRANG-JAY: Strang....

NATASHA: And now to the business at hand. I have decided as part of my new morals and ambitions that I must solve the murder of Lawrence.

REGINALD: But Lawrence killed himself.

NATASHA: Well then I must find his missing body.

REGINALD: But why Natasha?

NATASHA: Even after Death, some things remain intriguing. And now, I have this letter from Lawrence and I believe that there may be a way to decipher it. I am going to read it this Time with a pair of cryptic glasses I picked up at the Rebirth Conservatory that will reveal this letter's true nature and cause.

REGINALD: Give me that!

NATASHA: Never!

(NATASHA opens the letter and music starts. She suddenly has another very private musical moment.)

NATASHA: *(Singing)* No!!!!!!!!!!!
How can this be?
Why must this news come to me?
I must try to get it out
And let him know what it's about
But I don't dare....
I must love him more than I can bear.
I will feign confusion...again.

(Beat)

REGINALD: Well?

NATASHA: I still can't make heads or tales of it.

STRANG-JAY: Might I take a look?

NATASHA: Never!

STRANG-JAY: Perhaps my skills as an Inspector will come in handy Natasha.

NATASHA: Oh very well. Here!

(As NATASHA *hands the letter to* STRANG-JAY, REGINALD *is able to grab it and tear it up.)*

NATASHA: NO!!!!!!

STRANG-JAY: I say Reginald, that was thoroughly dramatic and somewhat out of character… Or was it?

(Suddenly UDI *and* ILYRIA *sit up, alive again.)*

UDI: Our Mastervork ees complet!!!!!!!

REGINALD: Udi! Ilyria! Are you both reborn as well?

UDI: Rebairn? Vee nevair died! In ze seatre zee artiste nevair dies, only leeves.

REGINALD: But I saw you die.

UDI: Ah! Vu saw zee illusion of Death. Vee cheve ben alive und vee cheve feenished our mastervork!

NATASHA: What's it called?

UDI: Za Deer.

NATASHA: The Deer?

UDI: Yezzz. Zo, zee truce ees eet eesn't called Za Deer, eet's true nem is "Domesticantala". Anychwho, vee ver tired of vaiting und taut eet time to pairform.

NATASHA: But events have just taken a turn of horrific magnitude.

UDI: Sounds like zee pairfect time for an interlude no?

STRANG-JAY: I say Natasha, it's fine with me to take an interlude. What do you say Reginald?

REGINALD: Perfectly fine with me.

STRANG-JAY: Strang—Very well then. Natasha let us get chairs for us and Reggie as well as Jacques Jacques.

REGINALD: For Jacques Jacques?

STRANG-JAY: Yes some time in the midst of this interlude Jacques Jacques will be reborn and join us as a spectator.

REGINALD: Why so?

STRANG-JAY: I don't know. I just know its right.

REGINALD: Fascinating.

(They set about their task while UDI *and* ILYRIA *start to set up, get dressed etc... A second later—)*

UDI: Vee are ready now.

STRANG-JAY: Pardon me before we begin Udi I must confess that I am stunned at Ilyria's blatant lack of dialogue.

UDI: Zee fair Ilyria chas decided as chev I dat ze Zeatre ees now her vun und only true luf und prefairs only to speak een zee pairformance.

STRANG-JAY: Very well then proceed.

UDI: Okay. Und now our masterverk "Za Deer" or eet's true tidal "Domesticantala".

STRANG-JAY: Pardon me Udi but might I ask, why two names?

UDI: Een za Zeatre da path to zee truce ees nevair seemple.

STRANG-JAY: Very well then proceed.

*(*ILYRIA *whispers in* UDI's *ear.)*

UDI: Yah, yah, yah. At zee request of Ilyria vee ask our kind audience to pleas refrain from any more quessions. Und now "Za Deer" or eet's true tidal "Domesticantala". Zee zetting ees a far off land in a different Time vare a man und vuman leeve een a small apartment und do zee sem routine every day. Day luf each other very moosh. Dare nems are Nancy, dat's Ilyria und Mick, dats me. Scene Vun. Dat night.

(Note: During the action of the play, time changes rapidly. Through the windows of the drawing room we are able to see it change from day to night to day to night, etc...at an alarming rate. At times the DEER *appears in the window and then disappears. Later, during* UDI's *monologue,* JACQUES JACQUES *is reborn and joins the others.)*

*(*Za Deer *or it's true title* Domesticantala *by Udi Bohe and Ilyria of the land of Ilyria)*

(Author's Note: The action of this play should be taken extremely seriously. These are real people going through real situations. They speak with American accents. It is the turn of the century. Which century is fairly obvious.)

(An apartment. NANCY *sits on the couch watching T V.* MICK *walks in.)*

MICK: Hey.

NANCY: Hey.

MICK: How was your day?

NANCY: Fine. Yours?

MICK: Fine.

NANCY: Hungry?

MICK: No.

NANCY: Me neither.

MICK: What are you watching?

NANCY: T V.

MICK: I can see that. What are you watching on the T V?

NANCY: Nothing.

MICK: Wanna have sex?

NANCY: Not right now.

MICK: Me neither. Tired?

NANCY: Yeah.

MICK: Wanna go to bed?

NANCY: Okay.

(For stage directions, UDI *steps out of character and speaks to his small audience.)*

UDI: Bleckout. Scen Deux. Vun minute later. Day are now een bed.

*(*MICK *and* NANCY *get into bed.)*

MICK: Goodnight.

NANCY: Goodnight.

MICK: Nancy?

NANCY: Yes Mick?

MICK: Do you love me?

NANCY: Yes Mick.

MICK: Good. Goodnight.

NANCY: Goodnight.

UDI: Bleckout. Scen Tree. Ten seconds later.

NANCY: Mick?

MICK: Yes Nancy?

NANCY: Do you love me?

MICK: Yes Nancy.

NANCY: Good. Goodnight.

MICK: Goodnight.

UDI: Bleckout. Scen Four. Feefteen seconds later.

MICK: Nancy.

NANCY: Yes Mick?

MICK: I can't sleep.

NANCY: Me neither.

MICK: Why can't you sleep?

NANCY: I don't know. You?

MICK: I don't know. What if I put on some music and we danced?

NANCY: Okay.

(MICK *turns on a small boom box and plays something.* MICK *and* NANCY *dance.)*

MICK: Did that work? Are you tired?

NANCY: No.

MICK: Me neither.

NANCY: Tell me every moment of your day. Maybe that will work.

MICK: Okay. I woke up this morning. Got out of bed. You were still asleep. I went into the bathroom. Used the toilet. Flushed it. Looked at my face in the mirror. I looked old. Then I made some coffee. I closed the bedroom door so as not to wake you and turned on the television to check the weather. It said it would be cold today. I thought that was funny because it was hot in the apartment but that the heat was deceptive. Then I turned on the computer and watched a music video. It was good. I don't know who the singer was. A girl. It was upbeat. Then I snuck back into the room and got dressed. You turned over in bed. I thought you were up. You said something I thought. I responded. You didn't hear me. You were asleep. I looked at myself

in the mirror again and wondered if I was getting
a second chin. Like my Father. A second chin and a
big belly. And hair in my ears. And I wondered what
I would die of. Stomach cancer, AIDS, heart attack,
Alzheimers, a car accident, a plane crash, murder,
suicide, boredom. And I thought about my skin getting
old and wrinkled and sagging and how I probably
wouldn't notice a lot of it at first and then one day I'd
wake and realize I was old. And then I thought that
it seemed impossible that I'd ever get old and then I
thought that death didn't sound so scary but it was still
death and then I thought I should stop thinking about
it and by then I was all dressed and I kissed you on
the forehead and you turned slightly and I walked out
the door. I went down the stairs and out the front door
and slipped on the ice and fell into the snow. I didn't
want to get up but I did. And I walked down the street
to the end of the block and I took a right and walked
four blocks to the subway. I got out my Metrocard and
swiped it. I have two days left on it. The train was just
arriving and I stepped on. It was so crowded. Someone
pushed me. I wanted to push them back but I didn't.
I couldn't get my headphones on so I just tried not
to think about anything. But I couldn't stop thinking
about what you said to me last night and how you
were joking but you really meant it and I wondered if
you really wanted to be with me or if you were with
me because I was easy to be with and that made me
sad because I didn't really know why I was with you
either. I didn't really know how I felt and how to feel
and if what I feel is love or comfort or if they're the
same thing or if one hurts the other or compliments the
other or complicates the other or kills the other. And
then I didn't care what it did because I was so confused
by myself. Then I got to my stop and got off the train
and went to work and nothing really happened there.
I did all the things I normally do . Well that's not true

I thought a lot about little things, you know like if
we should put more shelves in the living room or if
we should buy a new bed or if we should go away
to somewhere for a little while. Some place far away
and fantastic. A place we've never been before. But I
didn't know what that place would be because I didn't
want to go to any of the typical places like Paris or
London or even Budapest. I wanted to go somewhere
completely mysterious and unknown but I couldn't
think of any place on Earth that existed that was like
that. So I thought maybe we should just go to Miami
for a long weekend and lie on the beach and pretend
we were somewhere else. I went online looking for
cheap tickets but I didn't find any so I gave up and just
sat around and my office mate was talking to a friend
on the phone about whether to rent or buy and how
hard the market was and how it could be good to buy
in an area that's just coming up but if the area didn't
come up it'd be a bad investment and you could end
up living in the middle of nowhere. And I thought I
wouldn't mind living in the middle of nowhere with
no one around and no one to bother me and I thought
I'd like to disappear, become a ghost or a spirit and not
be seen or heard unless I wanted to be. And then the
day was over and I got back on the subway and came
home and there you were and here I am… *(Beat)* Did
that work? Are you tired?

NANCY: No.

MICK: Me neither.

NANCY: What should we do?

MICK: Let's hold each other.

NANCY: Okay.

(MICK and NANCY do.)

UDI: *(Now with true tenderness)* Sixty five years pess. Day steal chold onto each other. Und vun day day toirned eento and tree, entertwined togezer forever.

*(*MICK *and* NANCY *become a tree.)*

UDI: Und a Deer shtood under dare leaves und looked eento a chouse een anozer coontry vundering vat all zee commotion vas about.

(The DEER *appears in the window.)*

UDI: Zee end. Curtain.

*(*ILYRIA, UDI *and the* DEER *bow. Silence. No applause)*

UDI: *(Drained)* No comments yet please. Let eet's imagery seenk een. Ve vill tek und tirty second break und den meet in zee Drawing Room for a reception vare voo can geeve feedback.

(The two exit. Beat)

NATASHA: Oh Life! Fare. Thee. Well. Again. *(She pulls a vial out of her bodice. She drinks it and dies. Pretty much simultaneously)*

JACQUES JACQUES: And now I will stand here and stare off into the abyss of Life and Death.

*(*JACQUES JACQUES *does. Suddenly* REGINALD *grabs his head. There is nothing dramatic about it.)*

STRANG-JAY: You alright Reggie?

REGINALD: My head. It hurts terribly all of a sudden.

STRANG-JAY: Are you dying?

REGINALD: I'm sure it's just a headache. One can get a headache without dying.

STRANG-JAY: Yes I suppose one can though it is inherently not as dramatic as getting a headache and then dying.

REGINALD: I suppose.

(NATASHA *is reborn again.*)

NATASHA: I've been reborn. Again.

(NATASHA *stands next to* JACQUES JACQUES. *Then* UDI *and* ILYRIA *dressed up in all their finery appear. Ready to greet their fans. Unfortunately for them, no one seems to care.*)

UDI: Here vee are!

ILYRIA: Yes! We've arrived!

UDI: Anyvun wit comments about our mastervork can speak to us at any Time.

ILYRIA: Yes. We look forward to your comments as even though it is a masterwork it is still a work in progress.

UDI: Yezz, jus like Life!

(*No one responds to them.*)

UDI: I fear Ilyria dat no vun undershtood or liked our masterverk very moosh

ILYRIA: I can't truly say but I do know for certain that no one understood or liked our masterwork very much.

UDI: Eet ees enuf to mek me vant to die. Pairhaps den eet vill resonate!

ILYRIA: Oh don't die. Not today at least.

UDI: But vat should I do den?

ILYRIA: Well why don't we just hold each other?

UDI: Okay.

(*They do. This Time they really do become a tree. Right there in the drawing room.*)

NATASHA: Oh my, I'm so tired. Do you mind if I die for a little while?

JACQUES JACQUES: No go right ahead. Actually I think I may join you. Though I was thinking perhaps that I would die permanently.

NATASHA: I must admit. I've been harboring the same exact thought.

JACQUES JACQUES: Let's do it then.

NATASHA: Let's do it together!

JACQUES JACQUES: Very well... How should we do it?

NATASHA: What about Death by fire?

JACQUES JACQUES: Too hot. What about Death by accident?

NATASHA: Too haphazard...I know, let's just simply drop dead.

JACQUES JACQUES: I like that.

NATASHA: I as well. So simple. Shall we do it together?

JACQUES JACQUES: Yes. Together. On three then?

NATASHA: Very well. Three. Who should count?

JACQUES JACQUES: I will

NATASHA: Alright. Get on with it then.

JACQUES JACQUES: Alright. One, two...three.

(They fall to the ground. Dead. Beat)

REGINALD: I say Strang-Jay, are they really dead?

STRANG-JAY: It's really too soon to tell but by the power vested in me I now pronounce them dead and gone.

REGINALD: Would you get me a glass of water?

STRANG-JAY: Of course Reginald. *(He gets a glass of water from the wet bar.)* Here's your water.

REGINALD: Thank you ever so much. *(He drinks. Silence)*

STRANG-JAY: Well I suppose I should be shoving off. No more Intrigue or Death lurking around here. Only that damn Deer. *(He is just at the door when he stops and turns—)* I say though Reggie before I leave there's one bit of confusion I wonder if you'd help clear up.

REGINALD: Oh?

STRANG-JAY: That letter from Lawrence to Natasha. Why did you tear it up so violently?

REGINALD: What letter?

STRANG-JAY: The letter from Lawrence. Why did you tear it up?

REGINALD: Hmmm?

STRANG-JAY: Lawrence's letter. Why?

REGINALD: What's that?

STRANG-JAY: You're hiding something. What is it?

(Beat)

REGINALD: Damn you're good man.

STRANG-JAY: Aha!

REGINALD: Well Strang-jay, it's the strangest thing. You see Lawrence somehow got into his head that I was dying.

STRANG-JAY: You dying?

REGINALD: Yes.

STRANG-JAY: Why's that?

REGINALD: He claimed to have overheard a conversation between myself and Dr Favreau this morning.

STRANG-JAY: I see…. And did such a conversation take place Reginald?

(Beat)

REGINALD: No.

STRANG-JAY: I see…. Strang—and so Lawrence—

REGINALD: —was going to barge in and tell Natasha, so I killed him…. Accidentally of course.

STRANG-JAY: Of course…. So you tore up Lawrence's letter out of fear?

REGINALD: Yes.

STRANG-JAY: I see… Tell me Reginald, if indeed there was no conversation to be overheard between you and Dr Favreau, what were you afraid of? A lie?

REGINALD: Yes well as you know, the path to a lie is always simple.

STRANG-JAY: …Are you dying?

REGINALD: Me? Dying?

STRANG-JAY: Yes.

REGINALD: No, I'm perfectly healthy.

STRANG-JAY: Today yes.

REGINALD: Today and tomorrow and the tomorrow after that.

STRANG-JAY: But Death my dear fellow will one day take you.

REGINALD: Strang-jay, that is a figurative phrase. Death takes us all one day.

STRANG-JAY: Yes.

REGINALD: I'm not dying.

STRANG-JAY: No. But yes you are.

REGINALD: Yes. But only in the abstract.

STRANG-JAY: There is nothing abstract about Death.

REGINALD: Of course there is. Is Death at my door?

STRANG-JAY: Could be.

REGINALD: Do I have the symptoms of Death?

STRANG-JAY: You tell me.

REGINALD: I don't Strang-jay. It's pure abstraction. And now I will remove it from my mind. Be gone. There. All gone... And now if you don't mind Strang-jay I'd like to be alone.

(Beat)

STRANG-JAY: Very well then Reginald. I'm off. *(He starts to walk to the door. Just before he opens it—)* Before I go however I'd like to recite this final bit of information as straight forwardly as possible: Reginald I do believe that Lawrence had indeed discovered the truth.

REGINALD: The truth?

STRANG-JAY: Yes.

REGINALD: But why?

STRANG-JAY: I don't know. I simply know it's right.

(Beat. REGINALD *and* STRANG-JAY *stare at each other a moment. Then, something comes over* REGINALD *and he falls to the floor and dies.* STRANG-JAY *certain he has died doesn't know what to do.* REGINALD *then starts to laugh hysterically.)*

REGINALD: Just a little joke Strang-jay! Ha ha ha!

STRANG-JAY: I say, you did get my goat there old man!

REGINALD: Well what is Life if not for a joke or two, hmmm?

(Beat)

STRANG-JAY: Fare. Thee. Well. My friend. Fare. Thee. Well.

*(*REGINALD *and* STRANG-JAY *know this is a final goodbye.* STRANG-JAY *goes.* REGINALD *is alone. Beat)*

REGINALD: Are you all really and truly dead? Hmmm? Or will you be reborn any moment now? Natasha? Hmmm? Darling? Are you there? Can you hear me? This was all fun and games earlier but now it's simply

dreary. Do you hear me? Dreary. So come on, get
up off the floor and let's go up to bed. Call it night,
hmmm? Forget the whole day, start new tomorrow.
Come on Natasha. Get up. This is ridiculous. Does
it make you feel good to see me like this? Feeling
ridiculous? Answer me. Hmmm. Your silence speaks
volumes. Is there a secret in your silence? I think so.
Silence all around me. Silence and Death. Death. Ha!
Death are you listening? Are you there Death? Answer
me! Hmmm. Your silence speaks volumes as well. You
think you're powerful. All knowing. In control. An
intrigue. Well two can play at that game. I'll be silent
as well. I'll be silent as long as you are silent. *(He stops
talking for as long as he can bear)*. And how does that
make you feel? Hmmm? How does my silence make
you feel? Hmmm? Answer me? How does it make you
feel? How does it make you feel? How does it make
you feel?

*(The sun starts to set. It's slow and beautiful. In the window,
if only for a second we see the* DEER *looking in. Then all is
black. Out of the black—)*

REGINALD: Answer me. How does it make you feel?

END OF PLAY

www.ingramcontent.com/pod-product-compliance
Lightning Source LLC
Chambersburg PA
CBHW070031110426
42741CB00035B/2720